The Spiritual W

Glow Up Manual: Volume 1

God, Goals & Glam

Daily Affirmations to Help You Get Over Your Narcissistic Ex

Kill Jezebel Media, LLC
c/o C. Clark
PO Box 645
New York, NY 10272

ISBN-13: 9781717734655

Printed in the United States of America

Connect with the SWB

SpiritualWhistleblower.com
Facebook.com/SpiritualWhistleblower
Youtube.com/SpiritualWhistleblower
Instagram.com/SpiritualWhistleblower

This book is dedicated to my homies...

Kesha: *Thanks for being a real friend. You looked out for me when others wouldn't. You have always accepted me for who I am. You've never tried to change me or water me down. You allow me the space to be myself, but you're real enough to check me when I need to hear the truth. What people fail to realize is that a real genuine friend won't have you looking like a fool to the world. Here's to 20+ years of friendship and all of our talks about men. Love you Squirt! GSU I thought you knew, B*tchhhhh!!!*

Tamara: *I love your crazy ass. Thanks for listening to my late night rants. You are one of the few people who understand what Narcissism is because you've also been greatly affected by a Narcissist as well. Our stories are too similar girl. Don't ever change who you are to please no one! Your real friends will love you just as you are, just as I do! Remember that!*

Do not give what is holy to dogs, and do not throw your pearls before swine, or they will trample them under their feet, and turn and tear you to pieces

~ Matthew 7:6

God is within her,
she will not fall;
God will help her
at break of day

~ Psalm 46:5

The Spiritual Whistleblower's
Glow Up Manual: Volume 1

God, Goals & Glam

Daily Affirmations to Help You Get Over Your Narcissistic Ex

You cannot fix a broken man. He's damaged goods.

He will continue to repeat the same cycle of abuse with every woman he deals with and blame it on his victims. He needs psychological help, not your love and attention!

You are a diamond.
He didn't break you.
You broke him the
day you walked out
on him!

Get your Fuck boy Repellant ready!

The Narcissists are out this summer!

Side chick = Sanitation worker

Thank God for Side Chicks! They pick up your trash for you after you've disposed of it. The Side Chick did you a favor; now your ex-boyfriend can "stink" up her life with his cheating & lies.

He's her trash now!

God did not put you on this earth to be abused by no one.

Know thy worth woman.

The Narcissist sabotages all of his relationships. Be thankful he's gone.

He ain't gonna treat the next woman right either.

It's okay to cry. Get it out of your system, but once you're done, don't cry over that

Fuck boy ever again!

Any man that puts his hands on a woman, is a Bitch. He only bullies women because he knows he can't bully men.

Only punks do that!

Honey, you didn't just dodge a bullet. You dodged a WHOLE cannon ball. Be grateful to God that your ex is out of your life!

His stroke game is not all of that. You will see that once your feelings for him start to fade away.

Do you know how fabulous you are? He definitely does, that's why he's mad that you've moved on!

God does not bless mess, Honey. He pulled you up out of that relationship because He was tired of seeing His child being abused.

His mama crippled him. Let her have him. She thinks she's his wife anyway. So why compete with her?

Community dick is contaminated dick.

When's the last time you took yourself shopping?

Go again.

Girl, if you don't grow a backbone and leave that Fuck boy alone!

*Drop the clown and
pick up your crown!*

Psychological therapy is self-care.

Make sure that your mental health is top priority.

Schedule your appointment today!

When's the last time you signed up to volunteer for a charity or some other form of community service?

What are you waiting for?

You're lonely?

Buy a dog.

Dogs are loyal.

*Narcissistic ex-boyfriends
are not.*

An oyster has to be cracked open in order to expose the pearl inside. The same thing applies to you. Your breakthrough will come once you get rid of the toxic people in your life!

How much money did you spend on your ex? Just imagine how you could have invested that money on yourself instead.

Don't do it again.

Forgive him, but don't forget about the bullshit he put you through either. Just because you forgave him, doesn't mean he gets a pass to re-enter your life again! Protect your spiritual energy!

Your Narcissistic ex will call you a whore for dating a new man after you've broken up with him.

He can dish it, but he damn sure can't take it.

Mother made him.

Motherfuck him.

It's time to hit the gym girl. That cellulite is not gonna melt itself up out of your body.

He's mad that you're ignoring him? Well he should be. He ignored you during the relationship while he was cheating. He'll get over it.

The only way you can beat a Narcissist at his own game, is to not play his game at all.

Ignore!

They went out from us, but they did not really belong to us. For if they had belonged to us, they would have remained with us; but their going showed that none of them belonged to us.

1 John 2:19

Sis, there's no reason to stalk your ex-boyfriend.

He's repeating the same shit with his new chick.

He's still lying, cheating and manipulating!

Nothing has changed!

Be glad you don't have those problems anymore!

*A Queen doesn't allow
a Fuck boy back into
her life. She cuts him
off the first time she
catches him cheating.
The end.*

The National Domestic Violence Hotline is:

1-800-799-7233 (SAFE)

Have you written down a list of your future goals? Do it now.

Then plan to execute.

What's your credit score looking like? Could it use some improvement?

It's never too late to finish those classes. Go get that college degree!

Yes, your ex downgraded. What did you expect him to do? Are you really that shocked?

There's no reason why you cannot have the house or car of your dreams. Stop focusing on having a man and start saving your money.

Just remember that you deserve a real man, not a manipulator. You were designed to be someone's wife, not a doormat.

The only reason he's smearing your name to his boys is because he doesn't want another man to have you.

He's a Cock Blocker and a Hater. Remember that.

Your eyes need to be focused on your future. God will lead you into your new season of blessings if you stay the course.

You are blessed and highly favored.

Watch your life start to change for the better once you kick his sorry ass to the curb!

Yes your ex is jealous of you and your achievements. He has no ambition to accomplish his own goals and never will.

Can you believe that you were sleeping with the enemy all of this time?

Do you really think you can spend the rest of your life with a liar?

Think long and hard.

One woman's Narcissistic trash is another woman's sewage.

Your ex doesn't look so handsome after all, does he?

Now's a good time to start eating healthier.

Change your eating habits for the better.

If he cheats on you and gets caught, I can guarantee you he will do it again.

He'll just be more strategic the next time around. Don't go back!

He has Mommy issues.

R-U-N!!

You have no business fighting over a man if he ain't your husband.

A boyfriend does not deserve husband privileges! He has to give you his last name first!

Take a good look in the mirror. Did you forget how beautiful you are?

You wanna know how to get over a man real quick? Get money and flip it three times!

You can't expect a Fuck boy to act mature with you, when he's still breastfeeding off of his Mommy.

He who finds a wife finds a good thing, and obtains favor from the Lord

~ Proverbs 18:22

Stop trying to raise that Grown boy! He don't wanna grow up! You're not his Mother.

Just imagine how further you'd be in life if you invested all of your time and energy on yourself instead of keeping tabs on your ex.

Round up your friends and take a day trip to the spa for some rejuvenation. You've earned it.

Would you rather be broke or lonely?

Because you're gonna end up being both if you choose to stay with a Fuck boy.

He hasn't changed for the better. His issues require him to go to intensive

Psychotherapy.

(And you know damn well he ain't going to no therapy)

He's happy being a Fuck boy.

Move on and do better.

Poverty penis is not something that a Queen stresses over!

Ask God to restore your health and finances. Stay faithful and continue to work on yourself. He'll come through for you soon!

Stop having a pity party. You fucked up, so forgive yourself and start over!

Some men ruin good women because they secretly want to be with a man. Your relationship would have never worked out regardless.

Your ex is jealous of you. He's too weak to build a solid future with a strong woman. The man that God has for you, will build you up, not destroy you.

You're an angel.

*You're ex is a demon.
Angels don't belong with
demons. He'll drag you to
hell and keep you there.*

You're not delusional.

You're not crazy.

You're not going insane.

He's projecting his insecurities onto you so that you can feel just as shitty as he does about himself.

He's insecure because he knows deep down inside that you deserve better.

He rather waste your time to prevent you from meeting a guy who can do a better job than he can!

The right guy won't hide you from the world. Matter of fact, he won't hide his relationship from Facebook nor will he hide his phone. Men like this are dead giveaways and can't be trusted.

A man who lies to you while looking you directly in the eye, is a man who will line you up to get you killed with those same lies.

If he's over the age of 40 and still cheating on every woman he commits to, then it means he secretly desires to be with a man. He hates women.

Rejoice! He's out of your life!

HIV is the price you pay for allowing a Fuck boy to ruin your life.

Be careful.

You're too pretty to be stressed over your ex all of the time.

He's ugly and unworthy of being thought of.

Stop wasting your brain cells on a demon.

You will slow down your healing process when you grant your ex-boyfriend access into your life. Don't allow him to sweet talk his way back in.

Shut him down!

When's the last time that you stocked up on cosmetics and played in the mirror?

Emotional eating won't make the pain go away. However, working out in the gym will.

Go handle your business.

He's looking for a surrogate mother, not a partner. You need a man, not a Grown Boy with Mommy issues.

Now's a great time to book a girl's trip to Mexico for some sun and fun!

Make sure the next man you align yourself with,

is spiritually, financially and morally responsible.

A man who doesn't respect himself, will disrespect you repeatedly.

The only time you should treat a man out to dinner, is when you have his last name. Boyfriends should not be rewarded with husband privileges.

Acupuncture is a great stress reliever. Meditate and cleanse your body with turmeric & ginger tea. You'd be surprised at how well it works to alleviate anxiety!

Don't give your ex-boyfriend permission to make you feel inferior. That's called "Projection" and it's unacceptable!

Your greatest competition will be you against yourself. Stop focusing on what other women are doing. Insecurities are not cute.

On your first few dates with a new guy, if he tells you that all of his ex-girlfriends are crazy, RUN!

He's a Narcissist!

She is clothed with strength and dignity and laughs without fear of the future.

~ Proverbs 31:25

Every time you sleep with your ex-boyfriend, you allow him to exert his demonic energy into your vagina and womb. This is how demonic strongholds and soul ties are formed.

Sexually Transmitted Demons – STDs.

Stop sleeping with your ex.

Sis, he spends most of his time playing video games and texting chicks behind your back. Is this what you really want for the rest of your life?

Seasons change.

Fuck boys do not.

Get dressed up and go to the club with your girls. Don't let that cute outfit go to waste just because you're feeling depressed.

He's mad that you're dating again?

Who cares?

That's his problem.

Not yours.

You have one father. Your ex does not have the right to dictate who you can and cannot date. Especially when he's fucked half of the town and exposed you to several STDs!

Chin up, adjust your crown. Walk with authority and know who the fuck you are!

It's okay to join a Domestic violence support group. You'd be surprised at how many women are going through the same shit that you are!

Inspire and aspire to be great. It's never too late!

Pussy is power!

Use it wisely.

There's billions of men on this earth who would treat you a hell of a lot better than your ex!

Cinderella had the last laugh, and so will you!

A real man will work hard to buy his own luxury car. A Fuck boy will pick up women in your car and tell everyone it's his.

Real men don't use women.

Lames do.

Why would you want a man with no morals? That's like allowing your child to get away with calling you a Bitch!

Men are not science projects. Either he has his shit together, or he doesn't. It's not your job to clean him up. He shouldn't even be dating anyone until he gets his life in order anyway!

If he's broke, he shouldn't be out fucking. He should be applying for jobs! Broke in 2018, means bum with no ambition!

Yes you are the bomb!

Repeat it over and over!

Without God, you won't have any luck finding a good man. Put Him first and He will send you the right guy when He feels the time is right.

Hey Sexy, it's his loss!

You can't expect closure from a man who wants you to leave the door opened for him to come back. Slam the door in his face.

ACCESS DENIED!

*It's not fun to sleep
with one eye open
because you can't
trust your man.*

You escaped a Narcissist. Job well done…

Now go glow up on his ass!

It's not your fault that he's a womanizer. Blame his mother and his father. That's not your baggage to carry.

He's not a man of God. He's not spiritual. He's not blessed. He hates himself. He hates happy people. He doesn't want you to be happy. He's a Narcissist. Misery loves company.

Don't entertain that text. Nothing good will come of it if you respond to your ex. He's baiting you because he wants to push your buttons and tell everyone you're crazy once you do respond. Ignore him.

If you only knew where his tongue has been, you wouldn't want people to know that you dated him.

He's trash girl.

A Fuck boy will gossip about you to other men to ruin your reputation because he knows how good of a woman you were to him and he doesn't want anyone else to have you.

When it's all said and done, you'll be so mad at yourself for crying over him. He wasn't worth one tear.

If he doesn't love himself, how can you possibly expect him to love you?

Shopping for new clothes is fun! Shopping for a new man is even better!

Sis, there's nothing special about your ex. He was just good at creating the illusion that he was.

He's a magician.

Be glad you don't have kids with him. The break up would have been much worse!

He's bitter. He's mad. He's petty. His good girl is gone. He never thought that you would move on, but you proved him wrong!

You win!

Listening to Drake's music will prolong your break up.

Listening to Cardi B's music will help you celebrate it!

When God finally sends you a good man, you won't think twice about your ex!

Sis, he's not sorry that he cheated. He's sorry that he got caught. He's a Narcissist.

The best revenge is success. Your ex will not want you to do better than him… and that should be all of the motivation you need.

*A Queen doesn't waste
her time on a Joker.
Play your cards right
the next time around.*

You don't need to be friends with your ex. A real friend wouldn't lie, cheat or abuse you.

He's not your friend.

Friends don't abuse friends!

A Fuck boy needs to have multiple women texting him 24/7 to validate his existence.

A real man only needs ONE Queen by his side to help him build an empire.

Which category do you fall in?

The next time you date, please pace the relationship and keep your legs closed. A man that rushes things, is only looking to control you.

Dreams really do come true if you apply yourself and put in the work. Now is the perfect time to accomplish your goals.

A couple years from now, you won't even care if your ex is dead or alive. This is called "Indifference."

Keep progressing.

You can't expect a boy to do a man's job. He can't love you right because his parent's didn't teach him how. It's not your job to teach him. Let that little boy play in the sand box with the little girls. You need a man, not a Grown boy.

Behind your toxic ex, is his group of toxic ass friends. If they were real men, they wouldn't associate with an abusive clown. Always check the integrity of a man's inner circle of friends. It will tell you a lot about who he is as a person.

*You deserve a man
with class, integrity
and values.
Narcissists don't
have standards.*

Your ex is contacting you because he either wants sex or he either wants to push your emotional buttons. Bleed him dry. Give him nothing.

There was a time when men protected women. It seems now that men expect women to protect them. Or at least the Fuck boys do.

You can't compete with his Mama. She put claims on him first. He's a Mama's boy and he's gonna keep her titty in his mouth. Run!

Queen, life is all about bouncing back after taking a loss. I know you have it in you!

Why would you want a man that stalks women on Facebook all day? You don't think you deserve better than that?

You were pretty before you met him and you're even prettier now!

Diamonds are cultivated from extreme heat & pressure!

Pick up your crown from off of the ground and place it where it belongs!
You are a Queen.

Don't you ever forget it.

Made in the USA
Las Vegas, NV
03 October 2023